The Science of Education

Chapter 13:
The Learning and Teaching of Foreign Languages

Caleb Gattegno

Educational Solutions Worldwide Inc.

First published in the United States of America in 1985. Reprinted in 1987.
Reprinted in 2010.

Author: Caleb Gattegno

ISBN 978-0-87825-226-8

Educational Solutions Worldwide Inc.
2nd Floor 99 University Place, New York, NY 10003-4555
www.EducationalSolutions.com

Acknowledgments

This chapter of the ongoing treatise The Science of Education, has benefited from the great care generously given it by Dr. Earl W. Stevick who took upon himself to put right, the many sentences which betrayed the author's lack of mastery of the English language. To him goes a very friendly and big thank you. Also for his suggestions about professional matters beyond the author's experience.

In the preparation of the text for the printers, my colleagues, Yolanda Maranga, Marie Antoinette Auguste, and Dr. Dorothea E. Hinman as usual were most helpful. They too need to be thanked here.

- Caleb Gattegno

Table of Contents

Preamble

Since only awareness is educable in man, which forms does such an awareness take when the field is foreign languages?

To arrive at the facts on which we must dwell to understand the challenge we must develop the instruments of research which include a whole set of questions.

Since those who wish to acquire a language already know at least another one, are there features of this acquisition of a second language or L_2, which depend on those of the acquisition of the first of L_1?

Do we know well enough the acquisition of L_1 to decide the question above? or must we gain our skills as investigators of the acquisition of L_2 (*or* L_3 . . .) by improving those skills in working first on L_1?

Is there not an essential difference between both which can be placed in the fact that L_1 is acquired and learned but not taught and that the acquisition of L_2 is a function of all that which teachers and especially creative teachers, can do? Does not this last insight suggest that we separate our studies into:

- finding out exactly what we can learn about language learning by working with babies and infants engaged in that acquisition, and
- examining how we can be inspired to develop techniques and materials which take advantage fully of the above to serve the cause of teaching L_2 best, since normally acquiring L_2 involves a teacher?

Strictly speaking, the study of the acquisition of L_2 cannot be paralleled to that of the acquisition of L_1 precisely because a new set of variables is introduced by including all that which goes with teachers, teaching, curricula, methods, materials. But the situation is less hopeless if we develop an approach to the acquisition of L_2 which is subordinated to the actual learning by a person already endowed with all that which is represented by the work done on L_1.

That this can in fact be done is a triumph for the science of education which can produce adequate technologies meeting the demands of the "learning and acquisition" of L_2 based on those developed by the learners of L_1.

Let us clear first here the distinctions between our uses of the words acquiring and learning, a language.

Already in Chapter 3 "*Affectivity & Learning*," we concerned ourselves with the work done by the self in the encounter of the unknown. We looked at the four phases of learning when this meant more than the mere payment of a part of one's self, a fraction of the energy of affectivity, to retain an impact which though unknown to us is known to someone else. To these payments we shall give a name (arbitrary of course) and call *ogden* that amount of energy mobilized by the self to ensure retention of what the self cannot do by itself.

True learning has many appearances according to what the self does with itself to change time into experience and thus either produce an *objectivation* or energy coagulated and capable of maintaining itself indefinitely, or maintain a *dynamic* which can link objectivations or *energize* them temporarily under the guidance of the self or some input from outside or from one's psyche or from one's affectivity.

In spite of all the different appearances, it is easy to see that in all learning, the self at first faces an unknown and thus, because of that, hesitates and uses time to try to make sense of what mobilizes it and holds it during that time. Present in the now, the self receives energy and recognizes either some of its attributes or some of what happens to itself in its presence or contact. *Phase one* is made of all the contacts with the unknown, held as such by the self which in the meantime is objectifying part of itself under the impacts of the received energy or energies.

The self uses time in these contacts, and finds in itself the remnants of these impacts. They are then looked at for what they are and what goes on between them, objectifying the inner reality, which new gains more and more attributes, which tell that they belong to the self. This is *phase two,* which lasts so long as the self is analyzing, questioning, trying. When it recognizes that familiarity reigns and the unknown (which has now lost the attribute of being unknown) has become known, *phase three* makes its appearance, and is then seen as mastery.

The test for mastery is in the use of a preparation for an encounter with a new unknown. This transfer of learning is *phase four* and while it closes the previous cycle it prepares for the next learning.

The acquisition of L_1 will be the passage from not owning L_1 to owning it to a level equivalent to being able to express what one wants to say in a manner acceptable to others.

Acquisition implies many learnings.

To study that acquisition will mean in the case of L_1 that we start from say birth till such an age when we are satisfied this child can relate to others by expressing verbally his thoughts, feelings and circumstances.

L_1

Every one of us is an energy system endowed with receptors which can convey to the self either that energy has been added or subtracted from it, or that energy has been shifted within it from one location to another. The self is endowed with awareness, will, sensitivities (forming its sensitivity,) with vulnerability (i.e. a capacity to act on thresholds to allow or prevent energy to reach one,) with perception (i.e. the multiple recognitions of the attributes of the energies received or displaced,) with retention which will form the several sorts of memories we all know (somatic memories, automatisms, habits, trained conditionings, etc.,) with discrimination, with abstraction (by simply stressing and ignoring simultaneously,) with intelligence (the capacity to draw out of one's psyche means to meet challenges in some way other than those which present themselves spontaneously,) with patience, with persistence, with commitment, all of which are needed to learn anything and go on learning, i.e. meet the descending unknown.To observe and act on the observation; to note similarities and differences and to stress either; to be able to will the *same* alterations of any part of the system by judging exactly where in the soma the energy released or mobilized is quantitatively unique but met at different moments, all these are required by the self to do pinpointedly the smallest jobs which go to form the numerous movements which constitute the four phases of all learnings, hence are found on a number of occasions in the acquisition of L_1.

Because humans can call in deliberately every one and all of these endowments, they can achieve the complex, subtle and prolonged tasks required by the apprenticeship in acquiring any spoken language existing around them from the moment of their birth. Thus what they do can be seen as *doing the right things* which we should consider carefully, first, to arrive at some understanding of what all babies do to acquire their language, and second, to counsel us on how we could operate to help non-babies acquire a second language.

Already in *The Universe of Babies* (1973) we sketched a way to apprehend such a common feat, performed by babies everywhere. That sketch can be evoked here and perhaps made more precise in some respect. It consists first, in asking the question: "What can a human baby do on its own in contact with the energy of the soma and the various dynamics in the various organs?" and second, in separating two activities, one of which we called "talking," entirely contained in the individual baby and which must precede the second, which we called "speaking." This allows intercourse between a "talking baby" and its environment. This is seen as a verbal field in which a number of organized uses of energy are being selected with consistency to arrive at agreed conventions making possible their use by anyone for his or her own purpose but also accessible to others as is.

Let us first look at talking.

Talking

Let us agree that this word will be used in this writing to cover what any baby does in the field of sound production as well as what *he can do entirely by himself* and for which he does not need anyone else of the environment. All that for which he must accept full responsibility to himself.

Our idea that babies are helpless should not extend to areas where they alone have entry and can take initiative knowingly.

The common idea that words are the stuff of verbal expression should be replaced by one in which the reality contemplated is truly described by us; and the study of distribution of energy over time takes much better care of that. In fact, everybody knows that *in the beginning there are no words* and that that beginning lasts a number of months for all of us, generally more than 9 months.

Our idea that babies hear words first and try to reproduce them is utterly non-factual. Hearing needs to be educated before it can function on words and each baby does this work of education, *no one else does it.* For no one else would know how to do it.

A very important observation needs to be made from the start: our phonation system is voluntary and our hearing is not.

Another important observation is that we have been told — by our ancestors who selected some words in all (?) languages to indicate their awareness of themselves — that "looking" and "listening" are functions of the self in contrast to "seeing" and "hearing" which conveys that what was without has been allowed to reach us and be held within. The first two are deliberate, the last two relative and non-compulsory, as is immediately and easily ascertained by referring oneself to seeing beauty and hearing harmony. We may be taught to see or hear but not to look or listen. This we must do through the movement of our own will.

Each of us, in the intimate non-verbal language of awareness, has reached this conclusion about him or herself and the world, as soon as our sensory nerves have been allowed to be myelinized, three or four weeks after birth.

Before leaving these generalities and concentrating on "talking," let us ask our readers to connect with their own critical intelligence and put it to work at every point of this pinpointed study of how babies work using their mental and other powers, and which we all take for granted because they are universally available and, smoothly and effortlessly, take people to a place from which they display commonly visible and noticeable behaviors.

In my crib I was left alone so long as I did not cry for help.

No one had any reason to ask what I was doing with my time when I was calm and satisfied, dry and comfortable.

Still I had my time to my self. I could open my eyes and move them. I could watch my breathing and play with the flow of air my voluntary chest muscles could allow me to vary, I could be present in any one of my voluntary muscles and study the variations of the muscle tone which holds them ready and permit myself to concentrate on obtaining what I can perceive as being different or the same. For instance, that I can shut or open my eyes at will; that I can hold my head up; that I can turn my head, etc. etc.

What no one can see is that I note every one of my new awarenesses and that increases my experience of myself by letting the new be known and letting it integrate the old. That there is so much to do that I need much time for it by exercising my learning powers *all that time*. My waking time was needed to relate to the non-self while my sleep took me back to my self to sort out my retentions of the day and integrate what these were with what was already there. That in sleep I grew, and in wakefulness, experimented.

Thus I learned how to handle inner energy shifts and impacts of energy, knowing which was which.

For our purpose of understanding "talking" we do not need to be in contact with what all babies do with themselves during those many days and hours of early childhood.* It may suffice that we be alerted to the reality of learning in both sleep and wakefulness, at the preverbal stages.

The acquisition of L_1 is based on learnings which have their roots not in the environment but in the self at work. Until this is clear all efforts will only yield little understanding and even be a waste of time. Investigators of the acquisition of L_1 must, themselves, learn to work with the energies within and their various dynamics. Before we can enter into "speaking" we must master the processes which go with the awarenesses of the distribution of energy over time just as we did when we were babies.

Energy is the ultimate reality in the cosmos, which includes us.

Variations of energy generate the possibility of *the awareness of time*. This in turn places at our disposal a receptacle in which we can make sense of temporal hierarchies of energy uses which represent our experiments with energy. Thus if I can become aware almost from the start of all the possibilities of the muscle tone of my lips by affecting it deliberately over a certain duration and a succession of durations, I must wait till my teeth break through my gums, to work on how those affect the flow of air I put off. If I can affect my vocal cords and note how their state (a result of ordering their muscle tone to be thus or thus) affects

---

* c.f. our monograph *The Universe of Babies* Educational Solutions Inc. New York City, 1973

the flow of air, I will need this awareness as an instrument before I can combine that knowledge with a study of the conjunction of my acting simultaneously on my lips. My self elaborates instruments of study and then studies how to bring these instruments together to achieve more or something else, in analogy with the cosmos first making hydrogen and oxygen and with them later generating water. The latter is a possibility of the existence of the first but does not take their place; all can co-exist in spite of the temporal hierarchy establishing which came first to make the last exist.

Babies do all this work knowingly and deliberately, thus making us understand why babyhood is needed, why we are small and at work on what only benefits ourselves. All our elaboration is within and absorbs all our time.

Unless we use the lighting of awareness we cannot come to grips with the challenges raised here. As we said earlier, learning is equivalent to living, *to consuming our time (which is our wealth) to give ourself experience* which stays with us either in the form of objectifications or of knowhow which are dynamic. All this clearly is or concerns energy. As energy systems we have no trouble accounting for our growth which is energy added and taken from the store found in the universe around.

* * *

In the temporal hierarchies we must place first the acquaintance of the self with its sound production system. This, because:

- it is at hand,

- is permeable to the will which can give commands in the form of altered muscle tones, and then

- we can become aware of the consequences.

Breathing takes air through the larynx. Crying is one of its uses. Every baby may learn to modulate its crying, to prolong it and to stop it. Thus from the start we dwell in our throat and control it as well as the flow of air. We quickly learn how to make it loud or less so, finding out the exact mechanisms of that and therefore own it fully as well for any other purpose of ours which is not crying.

The important point here is to grant to babies their ownership of such a presence, conscious presence, in the various organs composing the phonation system needed to dedicate each part to the formation of specific and determined wholes integrating those parts. For instance, acting on one's tongue and one's larynx at the same time and studying their respective contributions to final products which encompass each of them separately and all the intermediate mixings of both. When lips are added, when the walls made of the cheeks, the palate and later the teeth, are called in, it becomes obvious that a whole spectrum of complex sound productions are available to every child who can then play variations on them. These are gratuitous combinations produced by the self mainly for its acquaintance with a given somatic system generated in utero and whose possibilities can only be known and assessed ex-utero when air can flow through the organs under variable conditions proposed by the self for that study and ending in a thorough acquaintance.

Endless hours are spent by the young child not yet 10 weeks old, say, to make sure that learning has taken place, i.e. that a mastery has been achieved which might make possible other conquests than sound production. Vowels are produced first. But for each a baby has to find exactly how it is made in terms of quantities of energy poured (or simply added) in the relevant muscles in order to remake them exactly, thus leading to an awareness of *sameness*. Once this is attained a baby can act on the duration of the utterance and how the somatic meaning of that sound shortened or prolonged, reproduced continuously or staccato. An alternative, open to all, is to produce a different sound and recognize it as such by the amount of energy affecting the various muscle tones of the muscles involved. As soon as two sounds are known for what they are from within and hence how they differ, a possible exercise is the production of sequences of the two, intermingled in various ways. The "algebra" present is acknowledged and leads to the awareness that say *ai* differs from *ia*, that *aai* and *iaa* are not the same, but that *iai* is unique and remains the same by "reversal."

As many vowels as wanted can be produced and such combinations and permutations explored without effort or tuition. Rather every child can teach himself all this without consultation with anyone.

Of course, a special awareness is needed for a child to hear his utterances and know them as his. Because it is easy it is done quite early, mainly because the energy of an utterance can affect one's eardrums. But in its nature it is quite different from the awareness of the sound production: only a fraction of the energy of an utterance reaches the ears. Attributes of each utterance need be kept in mind to ensure recognition. This a baby does by reproducing the same sound a number of times and affecting the productions with distinguishable properties such as durations and permutations and concluding with certainty that what he hears is what he himself does.

Educating one's hearing requires the presence of the self in both one's throat and one's ear and molding hearing upon uttering until such time as the mere evocation of an utterance triggers the evocation of what is being heard. From then on the self can use hearing as a monitoring system of his utterances and give his hearing all the knowhow acquired through the effects of the will on the voluntary system in his mouth and consider this a transfer of awareness.

Of course, this education will continue and even be available all one's life (in particular, when acquiring an L_2). It still remains that knowing directly through awareness of muscle tone variations is not replaceable by dwelling in one's ear, which is a transferred knowing,

Beside the ears, the whole bony structure in the head is also affected by the energy of the utterances emitted and a baby is aware of that, so that to reach pure hearing a movement of abstraction is needed. Most grown-up babies are unable to recognize their taped voice when this is audiotaped simply because the harmonics added by the echo chambers in one's head are missing on the tape. While we can all recognize other people's voices all the time we do not recognize ours until we work on this new demand and complement *mentally* what we actually hear. Our awareness through our throats knows a different voice from that gotten by our ears, at least in the single case of ourselves, thus stressing the profound difference of knowing language by ear and by uttering it.

The fact that musical melodies are also energy distributions over time but will reach first our ears before we attempt to voice them, while suggesting opposite connections, will help us understand the connections between uttering and hearing and hearing and uttering. When uttering, the self does two things: it is related to its intention, its project, *and* to the ordering of the relevant muscles to produce the equivalent of the project. In hearing, on the other hand it must surrender to the incoming flow of energies and their variations, letting them reach the ear and produce awarenesses which can be retained as objectivations or as time endowed with energy. A melody listened to, i.e. with a presence in one's ears to let the energy in, molds duration and thus can be retained as it affects the substance of our energy system of which our brain is a part. It is energy affecting energy. There is nothing to remember but all to be retained. No request to test its being able to be recalled, but a penetration of our substance which recognizes the impact as such and can recall that addition of energy. If there is something to be remembered it would be the circumstances of the addition. Otherwise it is known as one's own but not as one's creation, as received and held, as integrated, i.e. making one with oneself, but also capable of being separated and contemplated by the self. Thus awareness can work on itself and know its working and workings. In particular, note the nature of utterances and that of sounds heard and attribute the first to oneself or others and the second to others or to oneself. The details as long as they are energy distributed over time can be evoked, i.e. brought back to awareness as a delineation of the actual energy received and thus can be re-lived either actually in real time or virtually in telescoped time. A whole melody can be triggered by two or three of its notes strung together in a time sequence even though it is not actualized in real time. The connection of the self to sounds received is of the same kind whether the sounds have been uttered by oneself as by others. No effort to retain is needed or implied.

As the uttering baby knows which are the additional energies contributed to sounds by stress or intonation, he will know how to blend or to separate these components on a packet received by his ears from himself or from others. Exercises to ensure these awarenesses so that there is no doubt that some energies are acknowledged as either sounds or stresses or silences or intonations, will provide babies with the necessary experience to relate intimately and immediately with flows of sounds produced first by themselves and later by others.

An educated ear is necessary for a serious engagement in the study of the attributes of what one hears and babies work on such an education by themselves in close contact with the challenges, since no one else can help. Hence, they give themselves not only the instruments needed but also the vulnerability which makes them specially sensitive to the minute and subtle energy changes over duration, which can be short or long.

All this of course does not show but we can accept that it is objectively there if we ask:

- how could one do a number of these things otherwise?
- who could help a baby do it? (and find no one)
- how could we account otherwise for the fact that when things become tangible and observable, that they are there?

The mere fact that in the beginning there are no words and that genes cannot account for the delay of months before babies discover speech in the environment — and take a number of months to learn to speak — force us to look for deeper mechanisms in the mind and for certain kinds of experiences akin to the final results: a willed flow of words which are carried by one's voice which has a certain number of attributes that are individual and idiosyncratic and others which are collective and communal.

The first are taken care of by all the work done by babies under what we called learning to talk to which we must add the melodies of the spoken languages around the babies which, like those of music, are energy distributions over time, accessible to every child individually but resulting in a group carrying it.

As to the second, we find in the reality of the specific spoken language in a given environment, attributes directly reachable because they are energy — and sounds, stresses and melody are three of them — and other attributes which are arbitrary and cannot be known directly. These will require special functionings of one's imagination and intelligence, as we shall see when we consider "speaking," revealing new competences of babies overlooked for too long by students of early childhood and in particular, by those concerned with first language acquisition.

Often, perhaps usually or even always (a fact hard to establish) a child who has completed the learnings under "talking," invents his own language which displays all the energy attributes of a language found in his environment except that *none of the units* uttered is a word of the environmental language. The job of speaking clearly cannot be done by the child on his own. All he could invent and produce, he has, but the arbitrariness he used for his personal language does not cover the historic choices for words which his ancestors had reasons to select and hold to, over many generations. Although such children (and they probably are very numerous) could enlighten us on the origin and evolution of spoken languages, they personally have to give up their artistic verbal monument and use all their abilities to acquire the language of their environment. It is still unknown whether they are helped or hindered by such an abandonment of a fully constituted first language. Clearly for such children, L_1 should be called L_2, ...

Summing up: "talking" is that part of the acquisition of L_1 during which every child specializes a number of learnings which provide him with a vast number of inner criteria which ensure that he hears what he can utter and give him an intimate and immediate acquaintance with the various energy contents of what he hears, this because the learnings were deliberate, willed, acted upon a voluntary system located in the throat and mouth, reachable from within and guided by a vigilant awareness working on energy variations which go on also to form a system. This is normally adequate. Deaf people do not have access to it and do not form it although they are able to do many things (paralleling "talking") when talking does not require hearing.

From “Talking” to “Speaking”

Since babies are surrounded by an environment, generally a speaking one, and since they end up speaking like people in it, it has generally been accepted that children imitate speakers and learn in that way.

We shall not spend much time on this not very useful approach to the challenge. Since our understanding of the challenge has been presented in the section on “talking,” readers will relate to our challenge differently.

What is new in “speaking” is that children are confronted with the arbitrariness of the lexicon of the language around them. Being wise and expert they know that the reality of spoken words is only in the energy of the sounds in them and in the stresses, phrasings and melody which appear when words are polysyllabic, run together and used in sets. Words have *no* meaning of their own — as everyone will make sure by listening to someone speaking an unknown language — babies look for what makes sense to them and find that intonation conveys information about the speaker and his or her emotional states.

Intonation being a human component of languages and not a linguistic one, brings to the listener direct human information which later will be organized intellectually under categories such as: sadness, irritation, joy, satisfaction, doubt, bewilderment, etc.

There is need for a bridge between "talking" and "speaking" and to find it we need to return to babies in their cribs entertaining their production of sounds. In that area, they are consciously engaged in working out how to generate syllables which contain the vowels they already know and "con-sonants" which correspond to configurations of their mouths and can only be uttered blended with vowels (when the consonant is not a sibilant,) whether these precede the con-sonant or follow it. So one day when a baby is producing one of the syllables *ma, pa* or some similar pair which when repeated seems to be a word of that language (like mama or papa or dad) and if someone other than the baby monitoring himself, hears him, it is legitimate for that person who then calls the baby's parents to tell them "X is calling you." As the environment fusses over such occurrence the baby can make the observation not yet made, that he can hear, made by others, what he can make himself and then he can concentrate on finding in their flow of words these bits he can attempt by himself.

That certainly constitutes a bridge.

Now the baby has a reason for listening to the flow of words of others and to explore it for what he knows, while when he is alone he goes on with his own projects unconcerned with what others do. As his parents are prepared to echo his productions, every day more, he finds, as a reality, that they too can utter understandable sounds which for him present meaning as to their energy content.

Another proper discovery at hand is that in that field of flow of sounds *there are consistencies*. These are found in himself when he produces the same sounds or uses the same "algebras" denoted by the operations of *substituting* one sound for another, of *addition*, of adding a sound at either or both ends of a sound unit, of *reversing* a sequence of sounds, or of *inserting* a sound within a string of other sounds. But also he finds that independently of the energy qualities of voices, like pitch, timber, intensity, other people's voices carry something which will become more and more a reality provided this child uses a power of his mind called *abstraction* already known to him and used by him in so many learnings.

Abstraction (or the simultaneous stressing and ignoring of components in a perceptible situation) is certainly needed in order to give reality to that small proportion of the total amount of energy carried in a sounded word, which is the actual energy of a word, i.e. that of the component sounds in it and of the stressed vowel if ever.

Babies spend time now peeling words out of voices and when they meet sounds they themselves can make they keep them within one category: that of those "common to me and them." It is the time thus spent which will become a solid bridge, but is also a beachhead for the conquest of "speaking."

All this is, of course, only a beginning in the detailed study of how each of us manages to shift from knowing himself and what happens within, to knowing what others do in the field of language with a process which has a history and has evolved collectively over generations. But this beginning is promising and has allowed us to speak intelligently of a universe into which we were not able or allowed to enter using only linguistic concepts and instruments.

* * *

We need now to consider the approaches open to babies for the conquest of "speaking" the environmental tongue.

Speaking

We begin here too with a self capable of awareness. But it already has all the arsenal of "talking" at its disposal.

Providing oneself with *criteria* which take care of the arbitrary lexicon is the new challenge.

Consistency is one of these criteria. This has two contributions to make. First, it provides a solid basis for endowing words with a reality beyond their energy content. Second, on the basis of this reality it mobilizes intelligence to sort verbal problems which arise all the time.

We know from the studies on language made over the last few hundred years, that grammarians have classified words and defined categories about which we learn at school. Hence, we have *intellectual criteria* which allow us to distinguish nouns from prepositions, from verbs, etc. But babies don't have these verbal definitions. What they have are perceptions, sensitivities, retention; reflection on the compatibility or mutual exclusion, of observations on themselves and on what strikes them from outside; and a few other means which this study will reveal.

As sounds, all words are equivalent and we saw how abstraction works to get them out of the vehicles of voices. That extraction of words will become second nature after a sufficient time of practice which babies decide by themselves to be sufficient to ensure mastery of a processing of energy. The job of transferring that study for every word from the ear to the mouth will also take time, using the presence of the self in the ear to hold the extracted word and then its presence in the utterance system to add the specific modulation discovered over one's voice, requiring also a vigilance to ensure that such utterances are acceptable to the originators of the sounds heard. In this complex multiple presence of the self we have the secret of babies' success in learning to speak, for the linear succession of one thing at a time cannot possibly serve to solve the problems encountered. By accepting, as investigators of this field, that if more presences are needed they will be supplied, we give ourselves a more realistic basis for understanding that babies do not despair in front of the enormous challenges and do not give up; instead they are calm and do all that is needed effortlessly.

Thus, as commands are connected with intonation (which supplies one of the means for getting meaning) consistency of the sound "eat" with a situation in which feeding is the aim and can be perceived.

Consistency of the sounds "come," "go," "take," "hold," etc. within complex situations which repeat themselves and can be perceived specifically will modulate the reality around and suggest that when these sounds are produced they trigger the evocation of something of the situation perceived. For each of these inputs there will be associated in a child's mind a complex of inner movements which will be objectified with a certainty that takes deeper roots with each successful new encounter. Since language is recurrent, there will be plenty of opportunities to experiment anew and confirm a guess or an intuition which will become a criterion for future use of a word studied in this way. It is the set of associated evocations which will justify retention and the holding of a word as a summary of meaning. What seems to be a mere repetition is in fact a complex study of a fleeting and evanescent reality, in which there are a number of components. Criteria are formed all the time and are usable as soon as the examination of the variables involved has yielded the impression that what there was to know is known.

Of course, the mass of words to be extracted and examined would constitute an insuperable obstacle if there were not definite strategies and tactics, available to the self-taught baby. Already built-in in the words, by construction by the creators of this or that language, are principles of economy and recurrent criteria. Some of these principles are of algebraic nature and have been studied under "talking" and its extensions into "speaking," others are specific alterations which, like suffixes or prefixes, always point at specific modifications of some perceptible situation. Their consistency will not escape the vigilant learner who will find it very convenient and economical to generate in one go — in paying a single ogden — a host of new words while knowing how this verbal modification corresponds to any number of situational alterations.

In contrast with this economy there will also be a perception of the need for a large number of labels when there are no ways of obtaining one perception from another when both are singular. Nouns are as numerous as there are objects which can be isolated and labeled separately. Each part of one's body has been given a label and to use these labels will require payment of ogdens and repeated usage to make second nature the triggering of the two-way connection.

Hence, it is perceptible to fresh learners that words can be classified

- as objectifications which need to be held as they are and used as they are, or
- as variable objectifications in which the variable part conveys part of one meaning, and the stable part another.

Plurality, for example, is perceptible in contrast to singularity (and in some cases duality). With that perception goes consistently some impact on the word if that is the case in that language, or some concomitant presence of specific particles in other languages.

The creators of languages had to make decisions about as many matters as learners have when they enter those languages, to account for their perceptions and what came to them to try to convey them to others. Because there exist a number of choices for such ways of accounting, there are a number of languages and not only one. Because there exist a number of languages we can postulate a number of choices for their creators, by which to render their awarenesses of their perceptions as an economical system. For learners, the system already exists and they have to reach the criteria used by the creators to ensure that the system created satisfies the needs of the creators and is compatible with the real qualities of the inner lives of people. Compatible, in particular, with the weakness of memory, which does not easily hold the arbitrary and prefers to cooperate with intelligence to produce economical devices for the re-creation of parts of the system. Grammarians are those who have made themselves sensitive to these economical devices.

Babies do not have to please anybody. They seek what is truly accessible to them and what can easily be retained and made functional. When they have a feeling of a certain kind which also has a label in the language that is used by people around, they will pick it up in preference and use it as one of their first words. For instance, if they want to use an eating implement rather than be fed and there is a word in their mother tongue which can convey their wish, they seem to find it and use it at once successfully even if it is the first word of their mother tongue they ever used.*

Babies have now equipped themselves with the various abilities required —

---

* In fact, no one can say that there is one word which is the preferred first word for any group of children (in a household, an institution or a community.) Those children we studied came up with a great variety. It is for every one of the readers to gather his or her own evidence.

- to listen to others to find which of the words they use can be extracted from their flow of words,
- to analyze this flow in terms of energy,
- to transmute those awarenesses in terms of their own utterances,
- to be with these and be alerted to any noticeable discrepancies between what they can hear and what they can utter,
- to work on their utterances to make them resemble what they heard until they are satisfied they can put them out as their judgment demands, and
- make this satisfactory utterance part of their storage of words now in construction.

Clearly, these know-how resemble in nature those of "talking," but now a new element is added and that is the association of this emission with a grasp of when it is appropriate to make such an utterance. When this association is established for sure we say that it *triggers* an action, an image or a thought *and* conversely.

Triggers are mental objectifications which can be organized in hierarchical structures: those of "talking" being integrated in those of "speaking" and these integrating the former so that ultimately they are known by the self and received by outsiders as if they are one, and their components lost in the learning process which is now subconscious.

* * *

Perception of reality is also a complex set of experiences not all calling in the same workings of awareness. If objects can be isolated from each other, the focusing of attention on each of them will produce singular images one for each object. If labels have already been given to them and are called nouns, these refer to a process of abstraction of some property recognizable in objects and which is the support of the noun in question. Nouns refer to concepts which can accommodate the perception of one object, the unique one in front of us but which has many other properties ignored in the labeling. Thus all glasses, or all tables, or all dogs, etc., however different from each other in each class, are acceptable as representatives of the label. Babies, who practiced abstraction even before they were born, have no problem attaching a label to a perception while suspending their judgment as to its application to a very different perception which includes the labeled component. Of course, the creators of language had invented words as labels for objects knowing that they cannot produce an infinity of labels to trigger each time a unique singular image. They discovered in themselves *invariants* and it is these to which they gave labels. Hence, words by construction were to ignore a host of values of variables and only refer to a class or a category which could have as many members as wanted with as many other properties as were compatible with the existence of that referred to and asking of the evocation triggered by the label, only that it have, among its properties, the one retained for the label. All houses are houses, all cars are cars, etc. and no one is troubled when hearing such words and fearing that the image evoked will not coincide with that in the mind of a speaker.

That babies have endowed themselves for such a use of language as it was created, is easily ascertained when it is noted that two "errors" often reported about infants learning to speak, can serve to illustrate this grasp of reality. One is the immediate application to dogs (cats) of the label learned about one cat (dog) ignoring some attributes which when stressed will require one of two labels and stressing others which are shared by the two classes. The other is the application of labels like papa (or mama) — which refer to specific relationships not obvious to very young children — to men (women) not in that relationship to them.

Babies have so many experiences of vast classes of impressions including extremely variable ones that the existence of single objects, of particular ones, requires much more adjustment of them than an indefinite class. Indeed, being mobile and in an environment in which changes of light, of distance, of angle of sight, are the essence of being alive in it, no baby has ever had the experience of a demand on him that he should not note the changes: classes are the way in which reality impacts us. *Hence*, concepts are the natural way of responding to one's perception of reality. Hence, words by definition (for the creators and/or for the newcomers to a language) can only refer to classes of impressions. Babies know that and have no need to be made specially aware of that fact, except when there is a tension because of a change of rule as in the case of say, papa. It is much easier to be in contact with classes of impressions (which is true of all of us who are in time and can see *and* evoke visual images at the same time) than to *statify* anything, i.e. reduce to zero the time factor which permeates the whole of life. So babies don't make that mistake and naturally store dynamic classes of impressions for some of which their ancestors provided labels.

But, of course there are differences too, noticeable differences between labeling the sources of images (or objects) and other perceptible attributes of theirs, such as their distances, their shapes, the succession of the concomitant feelings, for which labels are found in languages and for which specific awarenesses exist. Hence we must grant babies endowments which make them alert to the spectrum of meanings when we talk of one reality called "words." These *inner criteria* are mobilized at various moments and they convey to the self awareness of what one day will be labeled by specialized students of language, called grammarians, such as adjectives, adverbs, prepositions, conjunctions, articles, nouns, pronouns, verbs. And within these, subcategories like personal, possessive, demonstrative, relative, interrogative pronouns, and so on.

The endowment we are talking of must be connected with concrete adaptations of the self to certain awarenesses which are experienced again and again since language is recurrent. To learn to speak is precisely to mobilize at the proper moment the total awareness which will tell the self that one is to use the word "you" when one is talking to a person while one is looking at him or her and referring to him or her. If this is recognized as happening to oneself there are plenty of opportunities to test whether the label is the one to extract from the speech of others and to be used by oneself in reciprocation. Babies watch others when they tentatively test their apprehension of the validity of their observation about a use of a certain word. The test is spontaneous because they don't yet know for sure, they have a need to know and must experiment in order to meet that need. Babies don't have to be taught to test; testing is a concomitant of their quest for the truth about the use of language in which they are engaged as soon as they made the discovery that the speech of those around them represents uses of themselves which save their energies, increase their efficiency in some areas, and the yields of their impacts on the environment. Because words refer to concepts and to classes of entities accessible to babies through perception and awareness of the perception, languages become part of their inner functionings: *adjectives* being accessible because they refer to perceptible qualities for which there are labels; *verbs* because they refer to actions or states; *adverbs* because they affect verbs in specific ways and couple with them; *nouns* because they are stuck to images; *pronouns* because they are economical in referring to indefinite classes and thus allow one to express many things without need for further qualifications which would consume time and making the holdings of strings of words more difficult; *conjunctions*, as needed to articulate strings with each other either to add them or to contrast them with respect to specific properties that can be isolated by perception; *prepositions*, as needed to locate more precisely in space and time, etc. what one's expressions are referring to.

No one needs to be taught that one is in space and time, that one is aware that the self is involved in the here and now in some actual or virtual activity, that one is imaging, or recalling an experience, or envisaging an action, on what and so on. Babies are endowed with all the sensitivities and the vulnerabilities which put them in contact with the flow of time (lived time) and what happens in it. Language has been created and is in circulation around babies, for all those things awareness can reach as separable in one's experience and thus possibly labelable. So babies' endowments encounter language via their perception of reality and realities, once they made sense of why labels exist. They can then embark upon the acquisition of L_1 as a systematic study in which they progress all the time and not simply linearly and steadily, but in sui generis ways decided by everyone separately and which is better described as empirical and exponential. The first involving many actual mental powers and the second — the cumulative effect of learning — which allows larger and larger chunks of language to be integrated over equal durations precisely because one has become aware of intimate and inner connections in the language studied. The sucessive quantum jumps young children demonstrate in their acquisition of L_1 are helped by their being aware that (the creators of the) languages allotted devices to the various expansions and that these are essentially algebraic transformations that are at the reach of babies. Retention is then easy and is permanent, because it makes sense and is true.

Babies do not have to do all the jobs of grammarians since they have no means or intentions of recording their findings and of passing them to others. But they use the same sensitivities as grammarians and reach the same conclusions about the language of the environment. They do it with an urgency and an involvement which helps them integrate their findings to make them second nature and thus be forgotten as separate events in their lives. Their memory of their learning becomes built-in memory, functional memory, the merging of the old with the new, all the time as one new functional entity.

All of us forget how we learned each bit of the language around us because we do not need to remember it separately. Not because it is lost temporarily or permanently, as when we forget a name, a date or an address, but because the effect of integration is precisely to make separatedness disappear and hence the memory of the item being acquired which then appears as part of us and immediately recallable.

Learning is the process stretched over duration, *acquisition* is its result. Awareness is present while learning and leaves the items learned when we say they have been acquired. In some areas the two labels (learning and acquiring) are interchangeable, in others they are clearly distinct and point to different processes and involvements.

The acquisition of L_1 is the outcome of a hierarchy of learnings. Since L_1 cannot ever be said to be totally acquired, what we are after here is the study of the actual overcoming of obstacles in that apprenticeship all of us went through to end up speaking our native language. It all seems to be done without any effort on the part of babies and infants, and is so because the movements of the mind are to acquire first the criteria which make sense of the challenge and then to practice the point at stake until it becomes part of one's psyche.

For example, being in time will help in noticing the alterations in verbs which refer to past, present and future while one dwells in the awareness of this quality of time stressed within.

Not all languages display awarenesses of moods, tenses, persons, represented by specific words or alterations of words. When these exist explicitly, there is something specific to attach oneself to, but if other items in sentences refer to these temporal alterations indirectly, deeper awarenesses are called for. But they too go on to form criteria, and babies who know that criteria are essential and need to be formed first will look for them. In some Western European languages there are many tenses in the various moods. To master them will require that one becomes aware that the triplet past-present-future can be referred to in the past or the present or the future, indicating up to 9 referentials which have not all been isolated and made into specific tenses. Some of these languages require personal pronouns and others can dispense with them by stressing endings and some others use pronouns in spite of some morphological changes in the stem, which make possible that pronouns are not used (except in cases of emphasis). Unless infants watch carefully how people around them make such changes and note at the same time which alterations aim at triggering the specific meaning, they will be in total darkness when hearing people use them in their L_1. If by watching carefully they manage to attain the required mastery it will mean that there are perceptible concomitants to help them reach such conclusions. Students of the acquisition of L_1 must find which they are, for each language.

Babies also would know that two perceptions merged into one can be separated and stressed separately. For instance, shoes can be brown or black or of other colors. An infant could reach the association of the name of the object to the shape or function of the object, and the attribute of color as a variable and find how each of these words is called in or triggered and conversely. Once attributes are perceived per se as existing independently of the objects to which they are attached in the experiences one is in, a study of how the words for colors behave becomes possible. For instance, that they exclude each other, unless a conjunction indicates their copresence.

Copresence is a criterion which triggers "and." Exclusion results from its absence as well as the perception and one day the word "or" will appear as referring to exclusion.

Because of the various perceptions and the original experiences which attach words to classes, babies know —

- that nouns refer to classes of objects which can be very dissimilar (such as "hats" are, for example,)
- that attributes (say of color) refer to classes tolerant of many variations for one label (all the reds or yellows) but associated in some specific ways to the labels for the nouns which indicate separable impressions which are merged locally and specifically in the case of the objects concerned. An attentive baby will not fail to notice his own working of abstraction (stressing and ignoring done simultaneously) and how it helps him know which perceptions trigger which labels. Practice, and the fact that functional language is recurrent, will provide the opportunities to find out quite early some of the behaviors of classes (a chapter of algebra,)

- that it is the perceptibility to them of this algebra of classes which they acknowledge when they give evidence saying, for example, "my red hat and my red purse" or "which shoes shall I put on today, the brown ones or the black ones" stressing either the transfer of the attribute "red" from one object to another or leaving the name of the object invariant and labeling differently the different attributes. What is at the reach of babies is this significance of transfer clearly connected with intellectual items coming into existence because the content of the mind is made of classes of interrelated impressions. The impressions are the realities which serve as support to the arbitrary labels which — because they become triggers of those realities — gain themselves a status of a reality, most adults believe words have,
- that the properties (algebraic) of classes are accessible to them at the levels these are capable of becoming criteria, i.e. can trigger definite movements of energy within. This is proved by the evidence one can gather by hearing young children use conjunctions; double adjectives (like "a sweet hot drink,") affirmation and negation ("this is soft, not hard":) easy triggering of antonyms (the opposite of _____ is _____) learned almost at the same time.

Babies and young infants recognize the need for *transformations* very early, when they meet possessive adjectives. For "my hand" which can be said by everyone must become "your hand" or "his hand" when referred to, and the change corresponds to a perceptible criterion. Watching the transformations leads to learnings which are valid in specific circumstances and retained within the effect of the circumstances. For each transformation in a language there has been a need felt by the creators of that language, and it is that need which will be acquired as a separate awareness by every learner. With such awarenesses will go the actualization of changes in the utterances which are experienced as consistent and required from now on. *Practice will make them second nature.*

Among the above awarenesses we include demonstrative adjectives and pronouns (of which there are four in English each referring to a unique criterion;) comparatives and superlatives; the need for adverbs to affect verbs according to specific perceptions; the stringing of as many attributes as qualitative adjectives as can be gathered in one synthetic perception of say shape, size, color, relative positions so that one can say with meaning "the large red rectangular box on top of the high, brown, round table there."

"Sweet and pleasing" can be two simultaneous feelings known as copresent though distinguishable and calling different labels to refer to, each triggering a specific impression.

"On top" and "underneath" are recognized as needed according to which object is referred to first. This also applies when a statement asks for both possessive adjectives and pronouns. Which we refer to first, is a perceptible criterion triggering specific transformations leading to the awareness of existing *equivalent expressions*. Thus: “this is your pen and this mine” is equivalent to “this is my pen and this yours” because they describe equally well one and the same situation except for the order in which the “pens” are referred to.

Transformations and equivalences are co-present and happen to exist in all languages because they are needed to account for the dynamics behind perceptions, perceptions of situations, involvement in them, choices resulting for the non-necessity of a unique involvement and so on. Entering L_1 requires that infants perceive first the significance of both transformation and equivalence as tools for grasping complex, changeable, real aspects, of their environment. Since they cannot be taught, we have to accept that young humans have the power of perception of these mathematical instruments without which it is impossible to acquire a language, here L_1.

That mathematicians were the first to write about these instruments, and use them in the literature, does not preclude that all over our earth young children had to become aware of them and use them empirically to integrate the attributes of L_1 they refer to. Young children had no reason to call in a second level awareness needed to isolate them and speak of them as we need to. But without the first awareness they would miss the nature of the medium of speech as available to the other humans around them and hence miss learning it and acquiring their L_1.

Involvements with awareness in situations will structure time in successive durations each leaving behind what we can call the “experience” equivalent to each duration in our lives. Hence learning is also structured by such durations thus making clear that we need time to acquire the content of the reality of L_1 and making plain that learning to speak one's L_1 may require many months of all of us.

What time structures is the actual content of the acquisition. This may provide (possibly) *a unique, ultimately describable, succession of learnings, applicable to all learners,* because of the nesting of the temporal hierarchies of the attributes: one not being able to be attempted before others have been integrated. But (possibly) no such unique succession exists and a common knowledge of language can be an unreachable reality. Possibly too not needed to account for all the individual acquisitions. We may arrive at the conclusion that a child has learned to speak his L_1 when his use of it, for his own expression, is of such quality that what he says triggers in others an understanding which is equivalent to the original, i.e. compatible through a certain number of transformations to the intention of the speaker, and as close as possible to what others would say in similar circumstances.

This is, therefore, a definition of *communication* as well.

Languages are not things, definite things, as much as they are sets of classes of entities linked by equivalences resulting from sets of transformations which objectify the dynamics behind the perceptions of a reality made of energies structured by durations.

However abstract this definition is, it is the one which best describes what babies have to contend with and manage to make sense of.

Essentially *energy and time* are at the origin of all realities.

Perception is the way the individual self relates to these realities. The truth perceived is therefore essentially dynamic: *classes* of impressions linked through awareness form the entities one's mind will entertain. The labels which are accepted as triggers of these entities and are retained as triggered for them, refer to classes of impressions. These classes are articulated by the self aware of items perceived as belonging to different classes at the same time.

We have not noticed that babies and young infants are sensitive to precisely these minute changes of energy affecting other minute amounts to which the self is attentive and can perceive more easily at the time in life when all is shade and hue, leaving for later contacts with larger amounts of energy. We have not stressed that words essentially refer to classes and — since we learn so early to speak our native tongue — that we must have been sensitive to classes of impressions before we gave ourselves mental entities which struck investigators in the ways objects do, particular objects which fill our field of perception and impinge on us through our sense organs. Philosophers and psychologists have taught us that our ways of knowing go from the particular to the general but never managed to make plain for us how this applies to learning a language. An apple is a singularly complex set of reflected photons varying with the incoming beam of light on it and with the angles they reach our retina, but we are satisfied by the statement "an apple is a fruit" using a more comprehensive class to serve as an indication that we understand the more restricted one. The particular is so much more complex and complicated than the general that we need many many words in a string to close in on the particular we have in mind.

It seems axiomatic today *that our epistemology to be correct* must begin with powers of the mind which remain in contact with reality from the start and that this reality is made of classes of impressions due to energy variations over time.

Hence the initial criterion which makes us capable of learning to speak is that of "rightness". As a learner I have no say about what I hear, it is sent to me as it is used by others and I have to receive it as it is. I strive to reach it as such and to mold my utterances on what my grasp of it is. To respect it as it is seems to come to me as soon as I notice both that the people around me can do what I can do and that they also do what I have not yet done. I will develop the sensitivity which will make me be impacted by the small fraction of energy that goes into the words in contrast with the considerable amount in the voices. By working on holding onto the impact in order to analyze its energy content and maintain its temporal structure while trying to translate such awarenesses into orders to my phonation system to produce an equivalent one in my utterances, I educate myself as a person observing precisely such structures. Fully engrossed in such activities my self learns to be effective in the complex in question. This takes on the form of particular exercises which make certain that I know how to do it until I have converted it into one of my endowments which will work automatically, no longer under the vigilance of my self but under that of my psyche.

Thus I teach myself first to be right. Rightness on any one word is then transferred onto a string of words, where new awareness may be needed taking on silences, stresses, blendings which can be seen simply as longer words requiring longer dwellings of the self on the place of impact as well as on the uttering system attempting to produce my own equivalent of what I hear. So "phrasing" will come into existence and when a few phrases are uttered in succession another reality is objectified which is called "melody" existing in the flow of sounds produced by others around me, which I let affect me as any melody because it is energy spread over time, but now will serve as a receptacle for a string of sounds I will produce. I have to be right on four counts: sounds in strings, stresses, phrasings and melodies, before my vocalizations will reflect those I hear from others. I shall therefore work on them deliberately only attempting that which I can hold in my awareness but which will become more and more as I work longer and more competently as a self-educated worker.

This realm of *rightness* only requires that I be sensitive to what I have to pay attention to, and *for that I do not need anyone else.*

I am an energy system endowed with awareness. Hence I can become aware of the energy inputs I receive and know them for what they are. But I am also aware of myself and all I did to my soma in-utero and since I was born. I know my will can affect my voluntary sound production system, and I can embark on producing what I heard if I know analytically its energy content, and until such time that my tests not only tell me that they are as I believe they should be, but also tell me how others will accept them as equivalent to what they produce. These tests are used by my self to shift the acquisition from full consciousness to my psyche, thus giving that acquisition the status of second nature.

Learning to speak is but one of the involvements of my self in the universe of energy. My perceptions are of all the changes in the spatio-temporal universe which reach me. I learn to use my hands to grasp more selectively, to help me to sit up, to follow moving objects, to focus my eyes and sort out shapes, colors, distances, relative positions, amounts of energy needed to hold, to turn and pull or push, to tear, bend, lift, throw, etc. At the same time to become acquainted with qualities of objects in terms of roughness or smoothness, softness or hardness, sharpness and bluntness and so on.

In other words, while I am working on acquiring L_1 in terms of the realities it challenges me with, I am developing the sense of meanings accessible in the universe around. Reaching "meanings" precedes my attempts at reaching "speaking" for the first are needed in the second. In fact, only because I have reached systems of meanings through all the awarenesses available to my self will I be able to retain the arbitrariness of the lexicon of my language. Words will be mine when I hook them onto my perceptions and the energies they mobilize. This causes their retention and the formation of the memory which will be termed "verbal". I will know, *because I did it myself,* that such a complex of sounds is to be triggered by such a meaning and conversely that such a meaning is to trigger that complex of sounds. Soon a new criterion comes into being to which we give a name of "*adequacy*". Every time we make use of a word or string of words and find that it triggers in the environment the response we had in mind, we shall pass that word (or words) *as adequate*. Once found adequate the pair meaning-word (or words) is shifted by the self to the psyche.

Together rightness and adequacy will give the green light to the functionality of the verbal expression to be considered as a means of communication with speakers around. It will be used first tentatively and when found valid, with confidence and without more presence of the self in it than is needed to push one set of words after another. *Fluency* is the result of work done on this kind of awareness of the self involved in such activities. There is not a single way of attaining it and observation of infants will produce a remarkable crop of ways indicating that the uniqueness of each human being translate itself in a multiplicity of acquisitions of the attributes of fluency.

Once fluent speech exists, it is permissible to the individual to identify with his or her power of expression which the will works for years maybe till the end of one's life. Those who try to become aware of the structure of their verbal expressions will encounter rightness and adequacy embedded in them. If they express their findings in terms of awareness of words and of time structures, they give verbal expressions a sui generis reality separated from all the work of the acquisitions which precede the objectification of a final and completed speech. These people become known among all speaking humans as specialists who call themselves linguists and grammarians.

"*Correctness*" is the term grammarians use instead of "rightness and adequacy" taken together.

"I'll see you yesterday" can be said; this statement has a structure identical to that of "I'll see you tomorrow" but it is not right because no one says it who knows the meaning of each of the words, and it is therefore excluded by the criterion of adequacy.

* * *

Armed with all the developed powers of "talking" and with those of "speaking" just surveyed, every baby who can hear and has direct access to meanings will embark on the acquisition of L_1 knowing that words are only one of its components, that the criterion of "rightness" is to be used all the time and that before words or phrases are retained, they must pass the test of adequacy linking words with the sources of *truth* and reality which are *in the perceptions of energy* and its changes over time.

Although it may be possible to outline an unfolding of the learnings which constitute this acquisition, its usefulness today cannot be guaranteed. We shall leave to the willing and industrious parents, the job of writing the monographs which describe the actual sequence of learning used by their offspring to endow themselves with the mastery of the language spoken around them. This collection will no doubt be full of surprises and will unveil much we cannot dream of at the present stage of our awareness of that field.

I know of two cases of boys who decided not to give evidence of their acquisition of L_1, who up to the age of four uttered no word and suddenly removed the censorship and spoke at once correctly and fluently, telling us that some of us discover very early that "virtual learning" is worth testing while most people choose "actual learning" with explicit corrective devices which do not need to be such for all.

L_2

The problem of the acquisition of L_2 is complicated, as we said, because there are teachers in the ordinary picture; teachers who are there in person in lessons, or through what they selected to put down in print to help students who purchase their works.

Whoever concerns himself with the study of the acquisition of L_2 will have to state categorically which are the guiding principles used in the proposals made. These principles must not be confused with a method which may or may not be made explicit and could well only be one of the possible actualizations of the principles. For example, the so-called "direct method" has a number of actualizations which differ considerably from each other, while all of them may stem from the same set of principles.

In this work we are concerned with the following challenge.

Having found in detail which learnings lead every one of us to the mastery of L_1, can we attempt to achieve a similar mastery of L_2 making use of that of L_1? In other words can we be inspired by the findings made in the study of the acquisition of L_1 to discover ways of teaching which *make every student of an L_2 reach the baby and the infant in him* and use its savvy to conquer swiftly, easily and for good L_2 almost as if it had become one's L_1?

This way of saying things may appear misleading and all those who teach languages know that for almost everybody learning an L_2 in later life (i.e. beyond early childhood) is anything but easy, swift and permanent. If we chose to say it in that way, it is because it seemed possible and it has been attempted a number of times with encouraging results. Here, we shall offer a proposal which takes care of many components of the situation even if a certain number are left out.

The value of the proposal may be found in that it is the first explicit presentation of *an epistemology of second language learning* which can serve those teachers who suspect that knowing what they are doing can serve their actions in the classrooms where languages are taught.

Our guide remains the study of the acquisition of L_1.

L_1 was first met as a spoken language. Can we use this encounter to present the spoken version of L_2 to students? This has been tried by some "direct method" teachers and found that they were not always successful. But the meeting of the spoken language in L_1 was first through the mastery of "talking" and this has passed unnoticed so far. So our question is rather: can we use the powers of "talking" brought by our students with them, to introduce them to *the energy distribution* characteristic of L_2? Moreover "talking" stresses the voluntary character of the organs of phonation and postpones the education of one's hearing until the self of the students passes the first know-how to their ears which then act as vigilant monitors of future utterances.

As teachers engaged in that first study (of the means to produce such awarenesses of the sound system of L_2, including stresses, phrasing and melody) we need to know the reality of the phonetics and phonology of L_2. It may happen (as it does in a number of pairs of L_1 and L_2, say English and Japanese) that all the sounds of L_2 are already part of L_1 and students do not have to learn to produce a new set of sounds. In fact, such study of languages leads to the discovery that languages differ little in terms of the sounds they selected to retain, but differ considerably in terms of other choices such as combinations and permutations of sets of sounds, in stress and phrasings and in melody. Teachers must scrutinize these components and be aware of them in a manner which ensures that they are complete, and find a way to present them so that they be met in students' utterances displaying the same "rightness" as users of that L_2 seen as their L_1.

The main difficulty in this presentation of the phonology and the phonetics of L_2 has been that language teachers have accepted the axiom that because sounds have to be passed on to students, teachers must put in circulation these sounds which thus reach the students' ears. From then on it is left to the student to do the work of transmuting what he hears into what he says.

The logic of this is impregnable. Only, experience proves that it is rarely possible for non-baby students to perform well through this device however often the teacher is ready to repeat the sounds. We even find people who spend years in environments where a certain language is spoken who still speak L_2 with words as if their composing sounds had the values of their L_1 and with no suspicion that L_2 and L_1 have different melodies.

Is this the result of the difference of the presence of one's self in one's ears and mouth? We already saw in "talking" that the ear is late to be brought in while the voluntary part of one's mouth could be activated soon after the fourth week following one's birth. If we mobilized in our students the "talking" part would we not link with the baby in them?

To have asked the question puts us on the track of discovering the means which *bypass heaving* and *go straight to the voluntary basis of speech*. After thirty years of experimentation we can now ensure that any student, willing to *play the game*, will achieve — as an entirely separate skill — a remarkable production of the spoken part of L_2. And this generally in about the first two hours of deciding to work to acquire a certain L_2.

The "meaning" of this activity is precisely the production of statements in L_2 making sure that the sounds are right, their blendings and stresses as asked for, their phrasings are indicated and the melody conducted. Because that meaning is precise and understandable, students find themselves absorbed in the game and satisfied that it yields enough for them to feel motivated to continue for say two hours non-stop.

The challenge of bypassing the ear has been met by creating an instrument called the Sound/Color Chart in which the vowels of L_2 are represented by rectangles placed at the top, the consonants are represented by rectangles below a horizontal line separating them from the vowels. Each sound has been arbitrarily associated to one color. Diphthongs are represented in other rectangles by two colors, the first to be uttered on top.

The Sound/Color Chart by construction contains all the sounds of L_2. The choice of the colors is such that for different languages the convention of a choice of one color for one sound is maintained. Hence comparing visually two such charts will tell at once —

- whether there are new sounds when we pass from one to the other,
- which sounds are the same,
- how many new ones will have to be acquired,
- how many vowels and how many consonants form the phonetics of these languages,
- that a bird's-eye view of the spoken languages exists.

Through the experimentation with a number of such charts, for as many languages, it became plain that the mastery of the correspondence Sound/Color is best achieved if vowels are worked on first. Since languages do not differ so much in their consonants (which will take less time to be mastered once the vowels have been,) in order to give practice in the correspondence Sound/Color in the case of consonants, as many syllables are formed as can be made.

There are as many ways of choosing the consonants to be presented as one wishes. This choice is left to the individual teacher who has mastered the Sound/Color correspondence in the case of his L_1. There are so many choices that no two beginning lessons need be the same.

A suggestion which has always been successful is to use the names of the notes of the scale (do, re, mi, fa, so, la, ti) to get seven of the consonants if they exist in one's L_1 which is now L_2 for others.

The job for a teacher is to show students that statements in L_2 can be made when they know how to utter the vowels and all the syllables which can be formed with each of the seven consonants as soon as these are introduced as the names of the notes. Little needs to be remembered. In fact, none of the statements thus produced requires to be held in memory. The purpose of the exercise is to practice "talking" in L_2 — at the level the students are at, at the present time, i.e. understanding what speaking is in their own L_1, and using such know-how to produce modulated flows of words not belonging to their L_1 but accepted to belong to the L_2 they intend to acquire.

With all the vowels and seven consonants, it is easy to get an enormous yield sufficient to give students a feel of L_2 as well as a sense that they are equipped to "speak" in it, in a manner easy for them and comprehensible to natives even when the converse is obviously not true.

In two hours generally, it becomes possible to equip students with the powers "to read color" and "to modulate their flow of words" to resemble what they would recognize as the L_1 (the spoken language) of the natives, now an L_2 they are attempting to acquire.

Equipped with this ability, two exercises present themselves:

1. a set of words in color in the script of L_2 can be presented to them and they can all be decoded and sounded right (except perhaps for a need for an indication of some stresses if they are not marked;)
2. this set of words can be selected to be the names of the numerals in L_2 and in a couple of hours numeration and even arithmetic in L_2, can be mastered.

Reading color will be available from now on and all the sets of words displayed in color on charts can be tackled independently by the students *who can make sure* that they can say them correctly as natives would, although none of them would trigger any image which corresponds to a meaning attached to each, as natives do.

But if the chart looked at is the one for numerals, it is clear that meaning will be conveyed by associating the Arabic numerals from 1 to 9 with these words. These Arabic numerals are now universally adopted (sometimes as a second system by the peoples who had their own in the past and still use it in their numerical transactions).

"Ogden" is the name we have given to the mental energy mobilized to retain an arbitrary sound or an arbitrary connection. One must pay as many ogdens as there are color rectangles on the Sound/Color Chart in order to master the two-way triggering which are at the base of the exercises on "talking" in L_2 Now we have to pay nine ogdens to retain the names in L_2 of the nine numerals for 1, 2, 3. . . . . 9. To ensure payment teachers will introduce each digit separately and practice the automation of the triggering as the set increases from 1 to 9 pointing in *any* order, at each numeral in each of the successive subsets formed. For tests a student responds to a name uttered by the class by pointing at the appropriate numeral. Conversely the class can emit the name of any numeral pointed at by a student called in front of the class.

Nine ogdens have yielded nine numerals in their digital form but also on the charts where the names are written in color in the script of L_2. Thorough connections and associations between the three systems (of names, digits, and written forms) ensue so that any one of them triggers the others.

In different languages the approach will be different and the number of ogdens paid variable; but once known, the system will provide students with —

- a vast number of strings of words they can produce with full comprehension and with as good a pronunciation as natives,
- the only part of L_2 in which they can use their initiative to do what they want knowing exactly what they have in their minds and how to give it the form natives would give it, thus demonstrating *autonomy* in a field barely encountered a few hours earlier,
- a chance of mastering an important chunk of L_2 which in the modern commercial societies is called for so often,
- a basis to transfer to L_2 years of study of arithmetic in their L_1 at the cost of a small number of ogdens for the names of the algebraic operations of addition, subtraction, multiplication and division, and fractions,
- a basis for an early study of how to ask time and answering it; how to ask for telephone numbers and making phone calls; giving one's age and address, also for a small number of ogdens for the linking words (pointed at either on the Sound/Color Chart or on word charts if these words-in-color are on them).

Such a curriculum for the first six or so hours on L_2 may not appear as necessary. It becomes necessary if we think of the students entering L_2 for say, one hundred ogdens. There is nothing comparable anywhere else. Since the chapter on numeration is part of all curricula we are only asking that it be one of the first to be presented. One of the benefits is that students' morale will be high and that they will feel motivated to pursue such profitable and enjoyable studies.

Another benefit is that L_2 will not appear as a "foreign" language but rather as another way of doing things known to oneself.

This can remain the case from now on, provided we develop techniques which are as effective in other areas.

* * *

We have been able to determine such areas, thanks to the discovery —

- of the notion of "linguistic situations" easily available with a set of colored rods, and
- the determination of a "functional vocabulary" for each language which both can yield the set of *all* the structures of L_2 and allows an entry into the "spirit" of each L_2.

The enormous advantage of these gifts to beginner students of L_2 will soon be appreciated.

We call "linguistic situations" those situations whose function is to make people speak. There are situations of different kinds, some are geometric, some algebraic, some arithmetical, and so on. Each of them is conducive to awarenesses which belong to those fields. But if they lead someone to speak about the matters of those fields, they can also be considered to be linguistic since they lead to spontaneous flows of words; specialized words in each case. Pictures have such properties.

If we want to control the vocabulary and do not want to have to give words which will be met again only occasionally, we may want to look for means which will easily display the framework of a language. We found that a set of colored prisms $1cm^2$ in section and ranging in length from 1 to 10 cm can be such means.

Thousands of teachers have adopted those sets of rods for the purpose of conveying easily and precisely what they have in mind. Here we shall only say that they are useful because they allow meanings to be made immediately perceptible and give a chance to teachers to introduce the functional vocabulary of any language.

Indeed, we all live in space and time, act on things and on each other; relate in many ways to ourselves: have intentions, doubts; sense likelihoods and probabilities; forecast and make mistakes, enter into activities, stay in them, finish them and so on. They are the frames of reference of our lives which form the receptacles for most involvements. We shall call *functional vocabulary* the set of words which are needed for any and all our involvements; and *topical vocabulary*, the set which supplies the labels for specific involvements not necessarily repeatable with any frequency. Topics are as common as the need for a framework, but they differ from each other and call in different sets of words. Both sets need to be acquired if one wants to use L_2 as if it were one's L_1. But for teachers, they can be distinguished by the property of serving to take students, as soon as possible, to a stage of competence in thinking spontaneously and freely in L_2. Moreover while topics may require payment of hundreds of ogdens to be retained, the cost of acquiring the functional vocabulary may be reduced to very few hundred ogdens and serve *all* topics. It is therefore a criterion of economy of learning which makes us choose to concentrate on the vocabulary concerned with the complete set of structures of any language.

Merging together economy, functionality, competence, frames of reference, structures, we become aware that there exists a reality which we call "the ___ language" (where the ___ is to be filled by words like English, French, Mandarin, etc.) which it is wise to give students of L_2 during the first lessons (around fifty) and make them feel they have been brought in contact with "the spirit" of that language.

On the whole, this contact with the spirit of a language has been left to chance and believed to be accessible only a long time after one begins the study of an L_2, to acquire it as a living language. But if we attempt to give it deliberately as soon as we introduce students to L_2, we find a radical alteration of the climate in the classroom and a keenness in the students to make sense of how people can apprehend their world (inner and outer) through premises couched in L_2 which are so different from those couched in their L_1. Languages differ in grammar because they differ in spirit. For centuries grammars were offered first but were assimilated by a fraction of those studying them, leaving the others baffled and despairing of ever becoming fluent in an L_2. Now, if we open L_2 through a stress on the functional vocabulary which makes one function in L_2 more and more freely, we state that a change of awareness of reality is needed in order to become like natives and to use an L_2 like an L_1.

Once it is understood that languages have spirits — and that those spirits are not metaphysical entities but awarenesses of why languages function as they do — the learning required in the beginning is of how we enter into contact with their reality. Each language will therefore challenge teachers differently and the first few lessons will be of greater importance than the following ones.

To objectify *the functional vocabulary*, and through it *the spirit of a language* — which is connected to the history of the group whose language we are studying — we display on wall charts, words colored so as to make their pronunciation accessible. A few hundred (two or three hundred) words, some of which can be strung together (with a pointer) allow us to produce sentences whose meaning is made accessible through situations with the rods which are unambiguous and therefore immediately meaningful.

Because the words (in color) are permanently displayed on the classroom walls, students can fall back on them and they no longer invoked having forgotten them. The fact that colors trigger sounds will also not require payment of ogdens for reaching how these words are to be uttered. Because language is recurrent, the functional words will be used again and again, and through that practice no one notices how the ogdens for them are being paid. Retention follows without memorization (this will be needed in the case of topical words). The work of the teacher who has reached the spirit of L_2 is in the construction of these charts. The items selected for them will permit the transformations retained by the creators of that language (in a remote past) to account for their perception of a dynamic universe around, and in them.

Charts for all languages are similar in that respect and observers will not see the spirit of a language unless they too become sensitive to it and are able to note how much language can result from such a small vocabulary. For example, for English, 42 words form the content of Chart 1. Still, it is possible to work for many hours with these few words and generate a tremendous yield which English-speaking people find illuminating and exciting although none of these words is, seen at first, other than ordinary and even be pedestrian ones.

Such feeling guarantees that we are in contact with the spirit of English.

There is no point in a writing as this one to refer to the spirit of a number of languages, for each of them may require a large number of pages. But in the space available we can explain how we unfold a sequence of lessons leading to a sense of security with the L_2 the class is working on, which by the nature of the exercises will also take care of the spirit of the language concerned.

The peoples whose language is being studied have made a certain number of choices a long time ago. They use or don't use declensions (from three or up to seven). They use or don't use articles and have one, two or three genders for their nouns. They use or don't use tones. They accept that some categories be invariable or make them all variable. They string words or keep them separate or sometimes do one and the other. They use personal pronouns in their conjugations or dispense with them. They use specific pronouns for every person or lump some together. They have or don't have verbs like "to have" or/and "to be". They use or don't use auxiliaries. They place verbs at the end or anywhere in a sentence. They have tenses and moods, a certain number of them or very few. They specifically indicate plurals or don't. They distinguish continuous quantities from discrete ones or don't. They play variations with special particles or have only prepositions and conjunctions. They need indicators with the numerals to specify quantities of different kinds while others do without them. They resort to specific means of economy to broaden the vocabulary, several of them of a mathematical nature, easily formalized. They, on the contrary, sometimes, resort to alternate means of handling a matter when others use only one way. And so on.

All these peculiar ways can be compounded producing still greater varieties of choices which characterize the various languages on earth. The earlier learners are acquainted with the choices which will define the L_2, the easier it will be for them *not* to fall back on the choices of their own L_1, thus avoiding the interferences of L_1 on L_2, often mentioned in the literature.

The exercises on the idiosyncrasies of the L_2 in question are those we concentrate on from the start and for some time.

By not using translation we stress —

- the separation of the learning of L_2 from the use of one's L_1, and
- the directness of the apprehension of the transmutation of linguistic situations into flows of words translating perceptions.

Because languages are concerned with classes and concepts, rendered by words, they call in essentially one's intellect. Speakers of L_2 (as their L_1) know themselves operating at an intellectual level but at the same time they have access to their feelings, emotions, perceptions and sense the impact of these on the selection of words to describe mutuality, exclusion, deference, manners, etc. So languages will also differ in such respects and it will be part of the encounter of of the spirit of L_2 to be made aware of their presence and their importance. Teachers may *for convenience* elect to stratify the early encounters with L_2 by stressing at one time only one of the social requirements of languages. But they must also, as soon as possible, bring in situations which will create a sense of the contrasts in relationships in the community (using L_2 as its L_1,) otherwise social complications may result. In the way languages reflect the "Weltanschauung" of groups (which we call their spirit) they also reflect social stratifications at this historical time. Learning L_2 is also acquiring a sense of how people relate to each other through their uses of words. These distinctions must be met rather early if not in the first beginnings.

* * *

Since babies can learn their L_1 everywhere on this planet, there must be criteria accessible to them for any language. Teaching of L_2s can then be helped if teachers learn to think in terms of criteria and conceive of their jobs as being the transfer of these criteria to their students.

There will be, within the broad criterion of rightness and that of adequacy, many more specific criteria to stress separately in the many lessons teachers will give their students. Rightness will be used as a framework for these new criteria which sharpen the understanding of how people speaking to each other (or sending the written forms of those speech acts to each other) convey precise meaning, i.e. what they have in mind and what are the triggers of their statements.

Learners will have to pay an ogden every time they want to adopt a word with at least one perceptible meaning as it is used by others. But they will soon find that the cost in ogdens is reduced because they can notice transformations (which the founders of that language retained as adequate) and dependent on intelligence rather than on memory. *The working of intelligence is not counted in ogdens.* Once we notice a regularity and test its existence in a number of cases, we adopt it for the purpose for which it was invented, i.e. the reduction of the burden on one's memory. Grammars offer these transformations as rules and propose to students that they learn them by paying ogdens for them. But babies — who are not taught — relate to them differently. They notice which part is steady, which part changes and what it is that requires that such a change be retained for the sake of rightness. Then it is the sensitivity to those circumstances which triggers the proper alteration on the steady part (or stem) for which ogdens have to be paid, (and have been paid). Such sensitivity is equivalent *to an inner criterion.*

Whether plurality asks for a change or not, requires a special awareness so that it either applies or is seen as not affecting a word, and the learner adopts this rule or these rules, knowingly.

A teacher working on language with deaf students (who do not have an *auditory criterion* of rightness) must perceive the connections above and invent ways of forcing awareness upon his students that such alterations are required in the L_1 of his environment — which is a non-spoken L_2 for them.

Grammar is of course implicit in the spoken language and will be made explicit by selections of exercises which force awareness first, and then provide practice by their multiplicity. Then these alterations become part of rightness and subsequently of correctness when isolated to be formulated as special requirements under specific circumstances.

In Russian, a look at a noun will tell whether it is masculine, feminine, or neuter, while in the Romance languages articles must be learned at the same time as the nouns, because very often there are no other criteria for the selected gender than that it has been chosen that way (sun is masculine in French, Italian and Spanish, but is feminine in German; the opposite is the case for moon).

Definite and indefinite articles, when they exist, can be connected to criteria which make sense of their usages. Such criteria need to be generated in the students by linking them to some perceptions. For example, in English when to use *a* or *the* may be connected to a perceptible attribute of plurality, but to shift from *a* to *an* or *thə* to *thee* as alternatives, is commanded by whether the nouns start with a vowel or not — a very different perception. In English, it is not *always* easy to decide whether to use the definite article or dispense with it, though in many cases there are perceptible attributes to guide the decision.

When confronted with such dilemmas, it becomes clear that there is need for criteria to form the foundation for grammar rules. When teaching the deaf this feeling is stronger still. The truth is that, when we pass on criteria to our students, they progress much more rapidly and safely than when we ask them to remember grammar rules exemplified by given examples. A good teacher is one who has found exercises which force awareness and thus generate criteria and one who makes sure that these are applied in all relevant cases — representing the practice which will make students assimilate the new criteria as belonging to rightness from now on.

Conjugation can provide such a set of criteria both when related to how words change with the subject (singular or plural) and how they change with the tenses or/and the moods. There is no real need to memorize paradigms. *Exercises stressing awareness* of who is uttering the word called a verb, or to whom it applies and to which time and mood one is referring, will suffice to provide the criteria exactly in the manner in which babies acquire their capacity to make such changes in their L_1

Moods reflect awarenesses of inner climates. Tenses do the same for an accurate placing of events on the time line. Hence creating linguistic situations — with or without the help of the rods — which convey certainty, doubt, commands or conditions, will take care of the ordinary moods of indicative, subjunctive, imperative, or conditional as perceived in the relationships of the speakers involved in the situations and in languages whose spirit has isolated them. As to tenses, action verbs force the awareness of the present, past and future, the latter attached to the intention to act, the first, in its continuous form, when speaking while acting and the middle one when the action is completed. Here no memorization is needed and there are very few ogdens to pay to master the transformations, at least in the case of regular verbs. Irregular verbs are handled through the additional criterion of rightness since it is not always possible to forecast the changes adopted by natives.

In ambiguous cases (found in many languages) students, like babies, will suspend their judgement until indicators allow them to make their up their minds and let a meaning settle down with an accompanying certainty for one choice of words. If this is understood by students, the frustration of being confronted with modes of thought different from the one their L_1 has formalized for them, will not take place. By the creation of situations illustrating the value of working towards being *patient* till one has criteria rather than by reference to contrasts with the students' L_1, teachers will convey their intuition of what needs to be done while helping their students find time to concentrate on the approach which L_2 provides for such situations. There are usually indicators to find, present in the sentences formed (if these are carefully chosen to display them) and students must learn to watch for them, as babies do, to make them into criteria. If ambiguities remain in some cases, there is need for more patience to receive at a later stage the indicator which settles the matter which is creating doubt. *Context* is the name for such a search for a missing criterion.

All languages require the use of context since people speak in the way they do when their thought is being cast on the spot and for purposes connected with concomitant experiences unsuspected by others. Languages are by definition to be used by many people whose statements are spontaneous and generally ad hoc.

Speakers work on their expressions and discover that there may be need for alterations to adjust to circumstances so as to obtain communication. Of course, there are many cases of non-ambiguity and these require little adjustment to shift from one's expression to one's communication. But there are also many situations which require discipline in order to reach a non-ambiguous expression.

Both are part of the use of language in social intercourse and both must be studied carefully. For example: "take two rods" is non-ambiguous as is "take two red rods"; the first conveys an agreement that from now on in this situation the color of the rods does not matter while the second conveys a greater specificity which remains in reserve if it is not used. By generating contradictions it is possible to create a context forcing some awareness felt as necessary. For example: "take two rods and give me the red one" may lead to confusion if no red has been selected while "take two red rods and give me one of them" eliminates the ambiguity.

Making students aware that expression is their responsibility and must be attended to carefully if communication is to have greater chances of happening, will be of great help in the mastery of L_2. Teachers paying attention to this hierarchy will prove to their students that they know where to work to use a language (here L_2) as means of communication. That communication has two ends and that everyone has to attend to one's own end (hoping the other will do the same) will create an alertness needed when the medium is words which by construction are made of classes which are indeterminate to a certain extent. When there is a perceptible context, it contributes towards making the words less crucial but since the aim is to use the language by itself, the linguistic situations with the rods will serve to make the words available at the same time as some meanings; and after that, for the words to trigger virtually those same meanings.

* * *

All the above does not tell which choices of situations and which classroom techniques will guarantee learning in every lesson provided the students either come motivated *to change their time into linguistic experience* or can be made to be motivated to do so. We can learn from the successful learning of L_1 by so many very young children, that there are things which can be done so that teachers only "do the right things" too.

One of them is to ensure from the beginning in a class that there is a *discipline of learning* and that students need to use it responsibly. This discipline demands *a presence* of the self which everyone can attain as a natural involvement in the manner we do when we cross a road in a place where traffic exists. Presence by itself eliminates distractions. The absence of distractions is an attribute of discipline. Students can reach in themselves what generates such distractions and how to stop them from reappearing so as to concentrate on the task at hand.

For example, when we use a Sound/Color Chart to present the phonetics of L_1, some students resist the fact that they are not given letters as they have come to expect a language to use a script for its objectivation. Even if they are told that all languages begin as spoken languages and only later are embodied in a script, their thought (or rather prejudice) prevents them from giving themselves to the task at hand. Anyone stopping, thinking, or checking the intrusion of the prejudice, will find it easy to concentrate on the job of associating specific sounds to specific colors and conversely.

Teachers will benefit greatly if they learn to obtain from their students those disciplines of learning which are demanded by the specific involvements which yield the awarenesses and the know-how that go to serve as springboards for further acquisitions of those parts of L_2 that the lessons concentrate on. When ogdens need to be paid, teachers must see to it that they have been. When sensitivities are too involved, teachers must make sure students are vulnerable to specific inputs of energy. There are suffixes and prefixes which when assimilated for what they allow students to do with the language, vastly increase their capacity to transmute their experience into the words of L_2. For example, the appearance of –ing (requiring just one ogden) alters radically what one can express in English. The right moment for its presentation and the manner in which its effect on verb-stems opens the articulation of a feeling of continuity in states or actions, will make students experience an explosion on their acquisition of English and a quantum jump in their learning of that L_2.

To make teachers sensitive to the small number of such explosions which cut into each L_2 large chunks so as to expose them to the light, will be one of the requirements of their education to learn to do the right things. Then their students will find themselves also being made sensitive to these vital transformations which stratify the course of study in major fashions.

Of course, there are many less spectacular advances which are also needed to be able to speak in L_2 about the visible and invisible relationships of items in one's environment. More ogdens will be required for these. We have here a measure of the importance of the awarenesses associated to various ogdens and we can ask ourselves whether we can postpone asking for their payment at a certain stage in a course. When we realize that a key word will be needed constantly we have to find out how to bring it in early. For generations, teachers may have been defeated by this challenge when they sensed they had a need for this key word but which they did not know how to bring forth since it was idiosyncratic in L_2 and not translatable except by a host of words in the students' L_1. Examples come at once to traditional teachers who find that "ser" and "estar," in Spanish, "en" in French, and similar small items in every language, remain beyond their skill of presentation, when in fact they are immediately made accessible through simple situations with the rods. Only sensitivity is required, sensitivity to the criteria which will trigger the proper word every time, as is the case with natives.

By clustering the functional words on (color word) charts, it becomes possible to convey to teachers a curriculum (one among many) by numbering a sequence of charts which are hung on the wall, one at a time, and unfold the curriculum selected. It is the responsibility of the maker of the charts to see to it that all the functional words are present or can be made with the parts presented. It is also his or her responsibility to ease the work of teachers by having criteria for clustering words so that as little time as possible is used to locate the words or endings needed. The various languages require a variety of beginnings, but all ask for one chart to start things off, with the presentation of enough to say (through the labels associated with immediate situations with the rods) and what can be done with them at once.

Since pronouns not only represent classes, like all words, but also classes of classes, they will be more frequently called in than nouns. So there are few nouns but *all* pronouns in Charts 1 and 2. A number of action verbs, most question words, all the conjunctions, a few adverbs, and some prepositions also come in these two charts. (This makes possible entry into hundreds and hundreds of complex, useful, current statements, which display the most useful, current, complex structures of the language.)

The vocabulary which describes spatial and temporal relationships comes next, making possible reference to the spatio-temporal frames in which all things happen, but now, with some precision.

Conjugations and most common verbs are presented so that nothing is left to be memorized but can be practiced asking for a certain number of ogdens, some already paid when studying personal pronouns (subject and object,) singular and plural and for the various persons (familiar and formal).

Generally, fewer than 200 or 300 words will take care of the structural demands of a language, but will allow generation of thousands of statements, the most important ones in terms of the structures of that language *and* giving the freedom of that language. Students will have this time to make sure that the functional vocabulary has become part of their flesh just as it is in their own L_1 and is spontaneously triggered according to the demands of the circumstances.

Because the functional vocabulary is so restricted, it can be mastered in a relatively small number of hours in class. But because it opens the whole of the language, it is unrestricted as the perpetual receptacle required by all statements to come when the topical vocabulary is bought at the rate of one ogden for every single object or special activity.

Ogdens are available in any numbers. Retention results both from the payment of ogdens and from practice. Man is a retentive system and there is no need to worry specially about forgetting thousands of words met in topical situations. If words do not come easily when needed, it is either because the payment of ogdens has not been attended to as required, or because the topic is not so frequent that it offers opportunities for reuse. Even in L_1 we meet the same lapses.

* * *

In the acquisition of L_2, we have seen the role played by all the valuable learnings of L_1 in making the task easier and also in generating the techniques and materials which will make study economical, effective, durable, and above all, functional and enjoyable.

The insistence on first acquiring the so-called functional vocabulary and later enlisting the words for the many topics (which constitute or open life of social relationships in a cultured society,) demonstrates our bias. Not one of our students will come to L_2 without owning an L_1. Hence it seems absurd not to secure "the _____ language" represented by the functional vocabulary and all that can be done with it as the safest entry into L_2 and see the rest of the work simply as expansion.

Collectively we have a long experience of presenting topics in L_2 and it is permissible to consider this challenge as much easier than the one we tackled systematically in this chapter. In fact, we shall not devote much space for this expansion and only say that a vast collection of pictures and books exists in quite a number of languages, to create an embarrassment of riches for all those who want to select their materials.

Of course, there remain problems for the Science of Education in that area too, but we leave them to other investigators.

To sum up this chapter devoted to what the Science of Education contributes to the acquisition of any L_2 or any number of L_2s, we considered first how we can handle the most foreign of all languages, viz. L_1. There our approach through awareness of energy and of energy distributions over time, gave us some fundamental insights into how babies learn and why in the beginning there were no words. The acquisition of L_1 occupied more than half this chapter and this was justified because it permitted us to grant young children all they did consciously and deliberately over a number of months after birth. This we called "talking" (for want of a better word) leaving "speaking" to refer to the apprenticeship of the objectified language in the environment of a "talking baby."

In particular the important thing to remember about the activities of a baby in developing an awareness of "talking," is that those activities do not present any mystery to him, and that these activities can be instrumental in bridging the gap to the conventional speech around him. Having recognized that words are arbitrary and that truth is met through perception of energy and energy variations, babies discover the truth of consistency. Languages are consistent and babies discover criteria in the conventions retained by those using words and groups of words, and transformations of words and on words, to refer consistently to items which are concomitant and perceptible.

Because of these functionings of their minds, children can enter the fleeting and complex universe of the speech of their communities and progress systematically as soon as enough safe ground has been generated by their activities, clearly intellectual, because of affecting classes and their relationships.

When at a tender age of two or three, a young child can express a host of inner experiences and test the good foundation of this verbal capacity, he can take it for granted and forget how he acquired his L_1. Perhaps using it implicitly when he learns to read and still later to write, his L_1. But when he comes, in later years, in contact with an L_2 through some teaching approach imposed on him, he may find himself *totally alienated from the competent learner in him.* The challenge of teaching appears differently to a scientist in the field of education. It can be defined by the proposal of *reaching the baby in each student of* L_2 so that the great expertise now dormant, can be used to acquire L_2 much more easily than one had done L_1. Indeed, a student who has done all the work of making sense of a process as abstract, arbitrary, conventional, embedded in L_1, will only need to apply that competence to cracking in L_2 even though differently, the way L_2 attacks the same challenges of life as in L_1.

Such an inspiration has permitted us to offer students of an L_2 activities which maintain: consciousness at the center; sensitivity and intelligence alert and present, and to recognize that there are:

- a receptacle forming "the language L_2," and
- a multitude of fillers which subdivide themselves into the words required by the various topics which make use of that receptacle.

Acquiring L_2 will then have two phases —

- mastery of "the language L_2" spoken, and written, and
- fluency on the various current topics, in L_2.

The Science of Education has already made possible the creation of adequate materials and techniques which guarantee phase one. It also developed a teacher education program which centers on the education of awareness and the development of the sensitivities of teachers so that they only do the right things.

Because this was the most urgent and seemed to be the most difficult to attain, at the present stage of the proposal, there is not as much to offer regarding phase two. Maybe what we have done in phase one will prove to be enough. But certainly in this chapter we have not devoted much space to it.

Each language being sui generis and asking for a special treatment, we would need a large number of addenda or appendices to spell out the contents of the word charts which allow teachers and students to tackle the idiosyncrasies of the various languages for which the work for phase one has been done to date. Readers will find a list at the end of the reference page.

Our awareness of *the subordination of teaching to learning* has led us to present to students, panoramic views of the challenges they have to meet and conquer:

1. the Sound/Color Chart gives a total view of the spoken language,

2. the Fidel; a total view of the set of graphemes-phonemes of the written language,

3. the Word Charts; a total view of the functional vocabulary and more, which provides a total view of what we call "the ______ language," leading to all the possible structures.

This is for phase one.

Phase two has no frontiers and a total view of it may be difficult to define. No presentation of it needs to be attempted outside the contents of libraries, the most comprehensive libraries at that.

In some of our writings, we considered matters left out here: composition in the various languages; assessment of progress and the use of other media are three of them.

Composition begins with the formation of a number of statements from the words contained on the word charts. Then it goes on by recognizing that some of these statements can be linked together to constitute a "story." Later, when contemplating pictures, one can use one's imagination to write a sequence of statements which can be read as a continuous narrative. More ambitious writings can be contemplated as the essential part of the work on topics.

A new idea about evaluation is that if teachers work to produce transfers of what is being learned, they can ascertain what the learning is and assess progress beyond retention of the content of lessons.

When contemplating the role of the media in the improvement of language learning and teaching, it was found that the maximal effect would be achieved when video is used to display learning as it actually takes place, rather than lessons taught by teachers.

The role of the computer in language teaching is still being investigated but no similar breakthrough has offered itself. No doubt that the powerful electronic instruments that are being developed will inspire some radical changes in this field, allowing us to take advantage of the attributes of these machines which are altering our lives.

Further Readings

Obtainable from Educational Solutions Worldwide Inc.*

1. *In the Beginning There Were No Words: The Universe of Babies*
2. *Teaching Foreign Languages in Schools: The Silent Way*
3. *The Common Sense of Teaching Foreign Languages*
4. *The Mind Teaches the Brain*
5. *The Common Sense of Teaching Reading and Writing*
6. *Towards a Visual Culture*

---

* Editor's note: Current offerings may vary. See www.EducationalSolutions.com for product details.

7. *What We Owe Children*

8. <u>Educational Solutions' Newsletters</u>

Vol. III, #1	*The Silent Way*
Vol. IV, #3	*ESL, The Silent Way*
Vol. IV, #4	*On Early Childhood*
Vol. VI, #4-5	*The Birth of the Language Video Project*
Vol. VII, #1	*Aspects of Language Learning*
Vol. VII, #2	*Further Insights into Learning Languages*
Vol. VII, #5	*In Favor of Bilingualism*
Vol. XII, #1	*The Origins and Evolution of Language Learning*
Vol. XII, #2	*Transfer of Learning*
Vol. XIII, #1	*Making Silent Way Materials*
Vol. XIV, #5	*The Silent Way and Zen*
Vol. XV, #5	*Can Language Teachers Be Open Minded?*

9. *"English, the Silent Way"* a video tape series, consisting of 140 half-hour lessons. Available on 3/4" U-matic NTSC. Also available in 1/2" VHS or Betamax on 35 tapes (each tape of four lessons).

10. *"Hebrew, the Silent Way"* a video tape series, consisting of 40 half-hour lessons, only on 3/4" U-matic NTSC.

11. *"Infused Reading"* a microcomputer literacy program also servicing to give rapidly an excellent command of pronunciation. Exists for English, French, German, Italian, and Spanish.

12. *Silent Way* materials

    Classroom: Word and Phonic Code Charts, 10 wall pictures, available for English, French, Iñupiaq and Spanish.

    Teacher: See #2 and #3 above.

    Student: *A Thousand Sentences, Short Passages, Eight Tales.* (The above books are available in English, Spanish, and French.) Minicharts for English, and worksheets for English, French, and Spanish to accompany wall pictures are also available.

13. *The Generation of Wealth* 1986

14. *The Science of Education Part 1: Theoretical Considerations*

    Introduction and Chapter 1: *How a Science is Born*

    Chapter 2: *Awareness of the Awareness*

    Chapter 3: *Facts of Awareness*

Chapter 4: *Affectivity and Learning*

Chapter 5: *Memory and Retention*

Chapter 6: *Forcing Awareness*

Chapters 2-5 have been made available as separate chapters since 1977, and can still be obtained in this form. They have been slightly edited for inclusion in the publication of *Part 1*.

Part 2 will be printed as separate chapters of which this is the first one: printed in 1985, and now reprinted 1987—

Chapter 13: *The Learning and Teaching of Foreign Languages*

15. Prototype classroom materials exist for —

    Arabic, Brazilian, Cebuano, Dutch, German, Greek, Hebrew, Hindi, Italian, Japanese, Korean, Lakota, Malay, Mandarin, Portuguese, Russian, Samoan, Tagalog, and Thai.

www.ingramcontent.com/pod-product-compliance
Lightning Source LLC
LaVergne TN
LVHW061225100826
845148LV00004B/862